Our Class Clothing Drive

Sharing and Re

I0804311

Sommer Conway

COMPUTER SCIENCE For the REAL World™

Rosen Classroom™

Our class is learning about reusing, or using objects again. We can reuse objects that we have to fill a new need.

We think about the objects we have at home. We think of jars, cans, books, and clothes. What objects should we reuse?

We have lots of clothes that don't fit us anymore. We decide to reuse our clothing. How can we reuse clothing?

Miss Held says we can give the clothing to kids who need it. Some people don't have the money to buy new clothes.

We make flyers to tell people about our class clothing drive. We ask for used shirts, pants, shorts, and shoes.

We tell all the teachers in our school about our clothing drive. They have adult clothing to reuse, too.

We send out letters to the community, too. We want our clothing drive to be the biggest one around.

Miss Miller's class asks if they can help. We share our flyers. They hand out the flyers in their neighborhoods.

We gather clothes in the school gym. There are tables full of clothes to reuse. Sharing flyers helped us gather more clothes!

Miss Held brings the clothes to a community center. They will give the clothes to people who need them.

Words to Know

clothes

flyer

gym